4

WHEN THE SAINTS GO MARCHIN' IN

Brightly

Traditional

FRANKIE AND JOHNNY

Moderately

Traditional

FUN WITH THE STRING BASS BY BILL BAY

NOTE: BOW MARKINGS HAVE BEEN ARRANGED TO SIMPLIFY PROBLEMS THE BEGINNER MAY ENCOUNTER AND TO DEVELOP THE DOWN AND UP MOVEMENT OF THE RIGHT ARM. PLAYING THE PIECES IN THIS TEXT WILL GREATLY IMPROVE BOTH RIGHT ARM SMOOTHNESS AND AGILITY.

CONTENTS

All of the solos in this text may be played *together* in *ensemble* with Fun With Violin, Fun With Viola, and Fun With Cello. Do to the nature of the upright bass, not all of the parts contain melody. Some of the parts need to be played in ensemble with the other string instruments to bring out the melody aspect of the song.

1 2 3 4 5 6 7 8 9 0

THE BASS

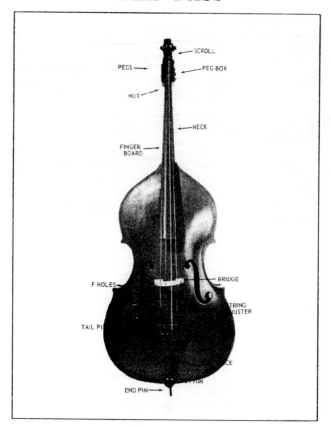

SCROLL
PEGS
PEG BOX
NUT
NECK
FINGER BOARD
F HOLES
BRIDGE
STRING ADJUSTER
TAIL PIECE
END PIN

THE BOW

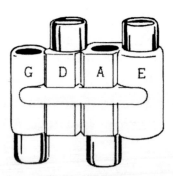

TIP
HAIR
STICK
GRIP
FROG
ADJUSTING SCREW

TUNING THE BASS

First String . . . . G
Second String . . . . D
Third String . . . . A
Fourth String . . . . E

Octave Below Middle "C"

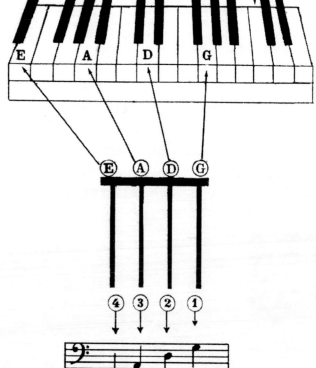

E   A   D   G

Ⓔ   Ⓐ   Ⓓ   Ⓖ

④ ③ ② ①

PITCH PIPES

G   D   A   E

A Pitch Pipe for the Bass may be purchased from any music store. Each pipe will have the correct pitch for each Bass string. A Pitch Pipe is a valuable aid.

BLACK IS THE COLOR OF MY TRUE LOVE'S HAIR

Stephen Foster

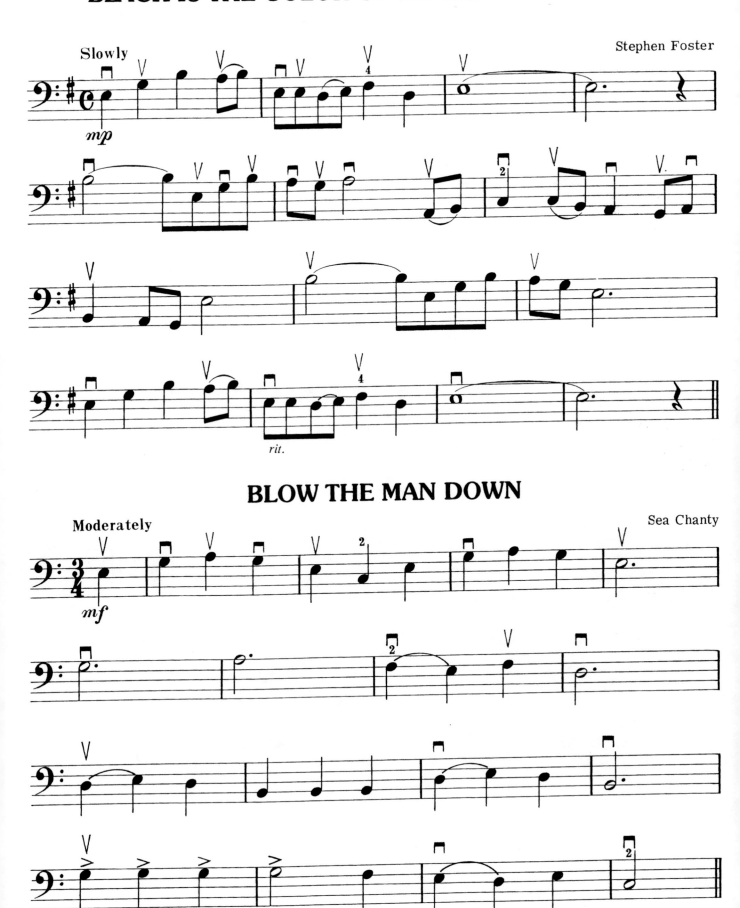

BLOW THE MAN DOWN

Sea Chanty

MICHAEL ROW THE BOAT ASHORE

RED RIVER VALLEY

DRINK TO ME ONLY WITH THINE EYES

Traditional

8

TOM DOOLEY

Folk Song

ALOETTE

French Song

9

AURA LEE

Traditional

STREETS OF LAREDO

Cowboy Song

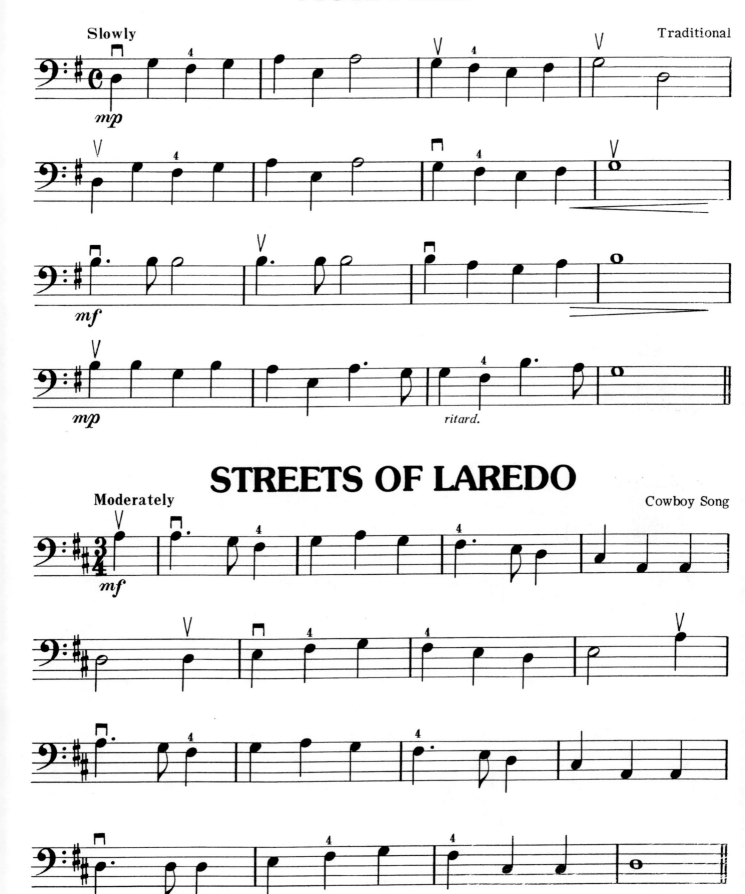

OH! SUSANNAH

American Folk Song

BLUE BELLS OF SCOTLAND

Scotch Folk Song

LOOK DOWN THAT LONELY ROAD

Spiritual

MY BONNIE

EYES OF TEXAS

Traditional

I'VE BEEN WORKIN' ON THE RAILROAD

Traditional

COCKLES AND MUSSELS

Folk Song

LOCH LOMOND

Scotch Folk Song

HOME ON THE RANGE

Cowboy Song

WAYFARIN' STRANGER

Folk Song

SHE'LL BE COMIN' ROUND THE MOUNTAIN

Traditional

GREENSLEEVES

Old English Song

HATIKVOH (THE HOPE)

Hebrew National Anthem

GYPSY LAMENT

Gypsy Folk Song

BILL BAILEY WON'T YOU PLEASE COME HOME

Dixieland

Bright, with a beat

BATTLE HYMN OF THE REPUBLIC

Julia Ward Howe

SHORTNIN' BREAD

Traditional

COME BACK TO TORINO

Francesco Carlo Zucco

Bright waltz

SWING LOW SWEET CHARIOT

SANTA LUCIA

Neapolitan Song

LONDONDERRY AIR

Slowly

Traditional

rit.

25

DOWN BY THE RIVERSIDE

Traditional

HAIL! HAIL! THE GANG'S ALL HERE

Traditional

DIXIE

Brightly

Traditional

WHEN JOHNNY COMES MARCHIN' HOME

Traditional

THIS TRAIN

Spiritual

28

DRUNKEN SAILOR

Sea Chant

I GAVE MY LOVE A CHERRY

Folk Song

IT TAKES A WORRIED MAN

Folk Song

THE ENTERTAINER

Scott Joplin

Moderately

SHENANDOAH

Folk Song

CAPE COD CHANTY

Sea Chanty

30

JOHN HENRY

Brightly
Folk So

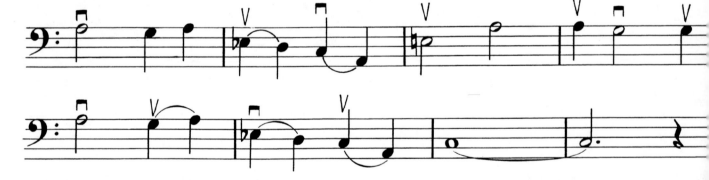

OLD SHOE BOOTS AND LEGGINS

Brightly
Traditio